PROTECTING THE NATION WITH THE U.S. ARMY

Rescue and Prevention: Defending Our Nation

- Biological and Germ Warfare Protection
- Border and Immigration Control
- Counterterrorist Forces with the CIA
- The Department of Homeland Security
- The Drug Enforcement Administration
- Firefighters
- Hostage Rescue with the FBI
- The National Guard
- Police Crime Prevention
- Protecting the Nation with the U.S. Air Force
- Protecting the Nation with the U.S. Army
- Protecting the Nation with the U.S. Navy
- Rescue at Sea with the U.S. and Canadian Coast Guards
- The U.S. Transportation Security Administration
- Wilderness Rescue with the U.S. Search and Rescue Task Force

RESCUE AND PREVENTION: Defending Our Nation

PROTECTING THE NATION WITH THE U.S. ARMY

CHRIS McNAB

MASON CREST PUBLISHERS
www.masoncrest.com

Mason Crest Publishers Inc.
370 Reed Road
Broomall, PA 19008
(866) MCP-BOOK (toll free)
www.masoncrest.com

First printing

1 2 3 4 5 6 7 8 9 10

Library of Congress Cataloging-in-Publication Data on file
at the Library of Congress

ISBN 1-59084-414-9

Editorial and design by
Amber Books Ltd.
Bradley's Close
74–77 White Lion Street
London N1 9PF
www.amberbooks.co.uk

Project Editor: Michael Spilling
Design: Graham Curd
Picture Research: Natasha Jones

Printed and bound in Jordan

Picture credits
Popperfoto: 24, 32, 65, 88; TRH Pictures: 8, 11, 12, 14, 15, 16, 18, 19, 20, 23, 26, 28, 31, 36,
38, 39, 40, 42, 45, 46, 49, 50, 53, 54, 57, 58, 60, 63, 64, 68, 70, 72, 75, 76; U.S. Department
of Defense: 6, 34, 66, 71, 78, 81, 82, 83, 84, 87.
Front cover: U.S. Department of Defense (top left, center), TRH (top right, bottom right,
bottom left).

DEDICATION

This book is dedicated to those who perished in the terrorist attacks of
September 11, 2001, and to all the committed individuals who continually
serve to defend freedom and protect the American people.

CONTENTS

INTRODUCTION

September 11, 2001, saw terrorism cast its lethal shadow across the globe. The deaths inflicted at the Twin Towers, at the Pentagon, and in Pennsylvania were truly an attack on the world and civilization itself. However, even as the impact echoed around the world, the forces of decency were fighting back: Americans drew inspiration from a new breed of previously unsung, everyday heroes. Amid the smoking rubble, firefighters, police officers, search-and-rescue, and other "first responders" made history. The sacrifices made that day will never be forgotten.

Out of the horror and destruction, we have fought back on every front. When the terrorists struck, their target was not just the United States, but also the values that the American people share with others all over the world who cherish freedom. Country by country, region by region, state by state, we have strengthened our public-safety efforts to make it much more difficult for terrorists.

Others have come to the forefront: from the Coast Guard to the Border Patrol, a wide range of agencies work day and night for our protection. Before the terrorist attacks of September 11, 2001, launched them into the spotlight, the courage of these guardians went largely unrecognized, although in truth, the sense of service was always honor enough for them. We can never repay the debt we owe them, but by increasing our understanding of the work they do, the *Rescue and Prevention: Defending Our Nation* books will enable us to better appreciate our brave defenders.

Steven L. Labov—CISM, MSO, CERT 3

Chief of Department, United States Search and Rescue Task Force

Left: A U.S. Army artillery sergeant stands guard at the 2002 Winter Olympics in Salt Lake City, Utah.

HISTORY OF THE U.S. ARMY

The U.S. Army has been protecting the citizens of the United States at home and abroad for over 225 years. From a tiny force of less than 1,000 men, it has grown into the largest and most powerful army in the world today.

The U.S. Army was created under the presidency of George Washington (1732–1799) on June 14, 1775, at the Second Continental Congress. The Revolutionary War (1775–1780) was just beginning, and the United States required a more organized military force to cast off British rule. As a result, the Continental Army was formed, commanded by a five-member civilian board. (To this day, U.S. forces are ultimately commanded by a civilian government to prevent the misuse of military power.) The army was small in size, initially numbering only 960 men, but alongside various state **militias**, it ultimately defeated the British at Yorktown in 1780. Its job done, the army was officially disbanded on November 2, 1783.

President Washington now faced a problem. The young United States still required a national army to protect it, but one that would not threaten the military independence of the various states. In the 1780s, the United States relied on state militias for protection.

Left: A soldier of the Honor Guard at Arlington National Cemetery, Virginia, marches in full dress uniform. The Honor Guard is a fully functioning infantry regiment, which conducts ceremonial duties within the Cemetery.

These militias had fought hard during the Revolutionary War, but they did have their limitations. Militia soldiers were mostly laborers, which meant that they could be called up for about 30–60 days only—any longer, and U.S. industry and agriculture suffered from a lack of manpower. Furthermore, the discipline and effectiveness of the militias varied tremendously.

These militias remained vital for the defense of the states, but the territory of the new United States was so vast that no single army could guard it. Washington realized that if the United States was to protect itself against the threat of invasion and internal conflict, and if it was to expand its western frontier, it needed a national army separate from state politics. So the U.S. Army was established, with Washington as its commander-in-chief. The state militias retained responsibility for their own localities, while the army was used to man coastal fortifications and open up new U.S. territories.

THE ARMY GOES TO WAR

The U.S. Army faced its first real military test in the War of 1812 (1812–1814) in which the United States fought against the British over territory and shipping rights. Though the Army struggled at first against the highly organized British units, it eventually proved to be a competent fighting force. Its numbers expanded from about 6,000 men at the start of the war to 33,000 by 1815. State militias (numbering some 500,000 men) did play a vital role in the war, but the Army often took the lion's share of the fighting. Its resilience led to a **truce** between Britain and the United States in 1814, and Britain finally gave up its attempt to influence U.S. affairs.

The Battle of Lexington (1775) was the first battle of the American War of Independence. Using accurate rifle fire, U.S. soldiers defeated a column of over 700 British troops sent by the governor of Massachusetts, General Gage, to seize a rebel outpost.

Following the war, the Army worked hard to improve the quality of its leaders. More officers were sent to the United States' first military academy, West Point, in New York, which had been established in 1812. Their skills were soon tested in another conflict, the Mexican War (1846–1848). In almost every major battle against the Mexicans, the Army was victorious. Its actions were supported by over 60,000 one-year volunteers from the various states, but its own size expanded to around 42,000 men. Despite the larger state force, the Army fought most of the major encounters and suffered over 70 percent of the total U.S. casualties.

In 1861, the federal army faced its most unpleasant conflict, the American Civil War (1861–1865). The Civil War was a war of the masses, and the scale of the conflict was so great that the regular army had a limited impact on its outcome. Over four million men fought, but less than 100,000 were U.S. Army regulars. When the war ended, the Army actually shrank in size, and by 1890, was reduced to a force of only about 27,000 men. It could be expanded in times of crisis by the reserve army, called the National Guard, but

The American Civil War (1861–1865) was the bloodiest episode in U.S. history, which left over one million dead. Regular soldiers were in a minority in the Union forces, but figures like Generals Lee, Grant, and Sherman demonstrated the excellence of the U.S. Army.

this was independent from the federal government. The drop in numbers and low morale in the Army led to high U.S. casualties during the Spanish-American War (1898) and the Philippines insurrection (1899–1902).

THE 20TH CENTURY

The first half of the 20th century saw steady changes in the U.S. Army. During the first two decades, its soldiers benefited from major leaps in military technology, including magazine rifles, machine guns, radio communications, new artillery, and the advent of military aviation. Officer-training schools grew in number, producing more men competent for leadership. Total soldier numbers grew to around 100,000 men by 1905 alone. Even so, the Army did not approach the scale of the major European armies, which were to face each other in World War I (1914–1918).

The United States did not enter the war until 1917, but even as battle lines were being drawn up across Europe, the U.S. government realized the importance of a large army. The National Defense Act of 1916 authorized the Army to expand to 175,000 men in 111 regiments. The National Guard, a special reserve element of the Army, grew to 400,000 members. During the war itself, the Army reached a total of 3,685,000 men, 75 percent of which were acquired through **conscription** under the Selective Service Act of 1917.

The U.S. Army fought with distinction during World War I. The war also saw the creation of the Air Service, an aviation wing of the Army. However, after the war, the Army, recognizing the need for better weaponry, logistics, and technology—and Army manpower

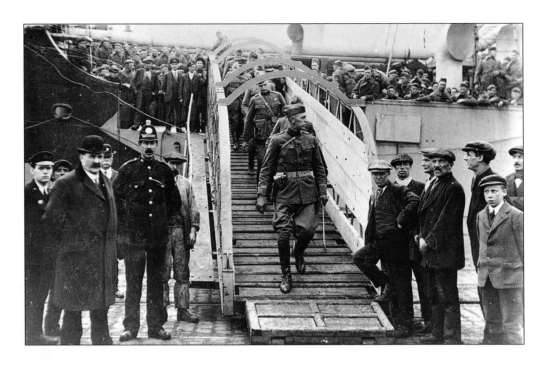

As the U.S. entered World War I in 1917, U.S. Army troops arrived in the U.K. ready for deployment to war-torn France. The influx of over two million U.S. soldiers led to a massive Allied advance against Germany, and the eventual defeat of the Germans the following year.

subsided to about 125,000 after the war. It was the next world war that would make the U.S. Army the most powerful force on earth.

The United States entered World War II (1939–1945) in 1941, but it began preparations for war at the outset of hostilities in Europe. In 1939, much of the Army's equipment was obsolete, and an economic depression meant that there were only 380,000 soldiers available. In 1940, the government made emergency plans to increase the size of the Army to 8.8 million in the case of war. When the United States went to war, the Army actually reached 11 million personnel, four million being ground forces; the rest were

ACTION ON OMAHA BEACH

On June 6, 1944, Allied forces stormed the beaches of Normandy, France, as part of a massive invasion of German-occupied Europe. There were five main landing areas, code-named Gold, Juno, Sword, Utah, and Omaha. It was at Omaha that the U.S. Army suffered a terrible slaughter. Omaha beach was six miles long and backed by 100-ft (33-m) high cliffs. The water and beach were heavily mined, and the German defenders were combat-hardened veterans. At 6.30 A.M. U.S. Army soldiers of the 1st Infantry Division and the 29th Division stormed ashore in assault boats into a hail of machine gun bullets and artillery fire; many were killed before they even stepped off the boats. Bodies soon littered the beach. Those who survived tried to find any cover they could. Finally, under the support of Naval bombardment, the U.S. soldiers inched their way up the beach and stormed the cliffs. The German positions began to fall, and by nightfall, the U.S. Army had taken the beach. However, they suffered over 2,400 casualties, nearly half of the total Allied casualties suffered on D-Day.

A wounded U.S. soldier is helped onto the beaches of Normandy, France, one of 6,000 U.S. casualties on June 6, 1944.

Sherman tanks of the 771st Tank Battalion advance through the battle-scarred German town of Muenster, April 1945.

split between the United States Army Air Force and the Army Service Forces. U.S. industry also rose to the challenge of war and began producing equipment in awesome numbers and superior quality. Without the Army's contribution, it is doubtful that Nazi Germany or Imperial Japan would have been defeated.

World War II turned the U.S. Army into a modern, professional, and powerful military force. The end of the war resulted in a plunge in numbers to just 554,000 troops, but as the **Cold War** developed, the Army once more needed to grow. The threat now was the Soviet

TESTIMONY OF RAY WELLS
COMPANY H, 141st INFANTRY REGIMENT

Ray Wells, a U.S. Army veteran of World War II and the Korean War, reflects poignantly on the personal effects of battle:

"I can only imagine what thoughts go through the young replacement when he reports to his company and sees what battle has done to the battle-hardened veteran. Many of these young men and boys, or most of them, rather, teenagers, never found their companies or knew a soul in their units, because in the heat of battle, in the dark, lonely and afraid, the enemy's bullet found them and they were no more. Perfect strangers to us. We sorrowed for these unknown comrades, but only their families, friends, wives, or sweethearts at home knew them. [We know] what battle and war really is, the sad, lonesome feeling of going back to the lines during the night, rain beating down on your face, fear in your hearts, and doing your best to not let the feeling [be] known to your buddies, and knowing that your comrades must be feeling the same way and would not let you down.

"I don't think I can really come up with the words so that the uninitiated can understand or even be interested, but I know the ones who went through these horrible experiences will understand what I am trying to say. Why were we, the living, allowed to come back; how were we chosen to continue with our lives when so many others made the extreme sacrifice and lie in those cemeteries, row upon row of crosses, so far away? God bless them and God bless all of you who are still suffering in your own way."

U.S. Army units fought in the Vietnam War between 1965 and 1973. The Army rarely took huge casualties in single actions, but suffered daily losses from mines, booby traps, and ambushes.

Union, and the war between U.S. **democracy** and Soviet **Communism** was fought in many different locations around the world. Within 20 years of the end of World War II, the U.S. Army had fought or entered into two major conflicts, the Korean War (1950–1952) and the Vietnam War (1963–1975). The constant commitments of the Army led to a peacetime strength of about one million personnel. Advances in the U.S. computer industry in the 1960s also let the Army lead the world in military technology.

The defeat in Vietnam taught the Army some painful lessons, because it bore a heavy share of the 58,000 U.S. personnel lost in the war. Since then, much of its effort has been channeled into peacekeeping and humanitarian and protective missions, though the Gulf War (1990–1991) and the war on terrorism in Afghanistan (2001–) have maintained the Army's combat expertise. Its soldiers, particularly those belonging to the special forces units, are regularly deployed overseas, protecting U.S. interests or democratic allies. Today's Army is backed by a current budget of $80.2 billion, making it the most financially stable and militarily advanced fighting force in the world. Though it has come a long way since 1775, the U.S. Army still has the same role: to ensure the peace and prosperity of the American people.

U.S. Army troops in Korea open fire with a .50-caliber machine gun. The U.S. Army led a United Nations peacekeeping force to defend democracy in Korea.

MISSIONS AND COMMANDS OF THE U.S. ARMY

The U.S. Army is a massive organization that needs strict lines of command if it is to function properly and efficiently. Ultimately, the leadership of the Army extends right back to the president of the United States.

The structure of the U.S. Army was established by the National Security Act of 1947 and its amendments in 1949. The 1947 Act altered the shape and composition of the Army. Most significantly, it transferred most of the Army's pilots and aircraft into the newly formed United States Air Force. The 1949 amendments set the relationship between the Army and the federal government.

At the top of the chain of command resides the National Command Authority, consisting of the president and the secretary of defense. The National Command Authority takes the final responsibility for U.S. military actions at home and abroad. The president is the commander-in-chief of the armed forces. He has the final say on the operational deployments of all U.S. forces—Army, Navy, Marine Corps, and Air Force. The secretary of defense exercises control over the Department of Defense.

Left: A soldier keeps guard during Operation Desert Storm, the Gulf War in 1991. The distinctive pattern on desert uniforms became known as the "chocolate chip" pattern by U.S. troops.

THE U.S. ARMY OATH OF ALLEGIANCE

The mission of the U.S. Army is best summarized in the oath of allegiance taken by all U.S. military personnel:

"I do solemnly swear that I will support and defend the Constitution of the United States against all enemies, foreign and domestic; that I will bear true faith and allegiance to the same; and that I will obey the orders of the President of the United States and the orders of the Officers appointed over me, according to regulations and the Uniform Code of Military Justice. So help me God!"

This oath commits the soldier to defend U.S. citizens and interests at home and abroad.

The Department of Defense has a vast range of roles, including:

- Developing policies that support the United States' security needs.
- Reviewing the condition of the armed forces and making changes to improve their readiness and capabilities.
- Overseeing the allocation of military budgets to the arms of service.
- Evaluating U.S. military actions and reviewing their accordance with national military and political objectives.

The next step down in the chain of command is the Joint Chiefs of Staff (JCS). The JCS contains the commanders of all four services: Army, Navy, Marine Corps, and Air Force. It receives the

The U.S. Army trains its soldiers to fight in any environment and any climate. Here, M60 tanks are practicing winter warfare tactics. The tanks have been painted in winter camouflage to break up their silhouettes against the snowy and mountainous background.

orders and recommendations of the secretary of defense and turns them into strategic goals for the armed forces. The military departments are responsible for training and equipping the armed forces and ensuring that they are ready for operations. Finally, the Unified Commands are the parts of the armed forces that actually conduct operations. A Unified Command consists of two or more services working together, usually within a designated geographical region, known as an "Area of Responsibility" (AoR). The AoR, for example, of the United States European Command covers 13 million square miles (34 million sq km) and 91 countries, from Norway in

General Peter Pace is the Vice-Chairman of the Joint Chiefs of Staff. As such, he is the second highest-ranking military officer in the United States, and exercises jurisdiction over all U.S. armed forces, including the Army.

northern Europe, down to the Cape of Good Hope in South Africa. The U.S. Army is present in each Unified Command, and its deployments reach worldwide, from Germany to Guam.

MISSIONS AND MAJOR COMMANDS

If need be, U.S. Army soldiers must be prepared to go to war and risk their own lives for the preservation of U.S. values and the American way of life, as has most recently been seen in the war on terrorism in Afghanistan. However, there are many other types of missions performed by the U.S. Army. It also gives federal, state, and local government agencies military assistance when required; conducts programs of environmental protection and development; acts as a relief force in times of natural disaster (including foreign disasters); conducts humanitarian or peacekeeping operations in accordance with its U.S., **NATO**, or **UN** responsibilities; also provides emergency medical air transportation.

All of these responsibilities are conducted under the authority of the Army's Major Commands. Major Commands are the subdivisions of the Army that control all aspects of Army training and operations. Currently, there are 15 Major Commands in the U.S. Army, each with its own distinct mission and program. Here, we will look at each Major Command in turn, noting its role and jurisdiction within the U.S. Army.

U.S. Army Europe (USAREUR)

USAREUR trains, prepares, and deploys a combat-ready military force of over 50,000 troops throughout Europe, Africa, and much of the Middle East. Its missions include providing and sustaining trained and ready forces, promoting regional stability, gathering intelligence, and conducting operations and exercises in the region. USAREUR's headquarters are in Stuttgart, Germany.

U.S. Army Forces Command (FORSCOM)

FORSCOM is the U.S. Army's largest Major Command. It is actually a part of the U.S. armed forces' Atlantic Command, but sends its soldiers to all worldwide destinations where they are needed.

Both the U.S. Army and U.S. Marine Corps use the M1 Abrams tank, the finest Main Battle Tank (MBT) in the world. The job of acquiring, evaluating, and authorizing U.S. Army technology falls to the Army Materiel Command (AMC) based in Arlington, Virginia.

FORSCOM controls some 760,000 regular soldiers, reservists, and National Guardsmen, and trains, mobilizes, and deploys them as required. Its headquarters are at Fort McPherson, Georgia.

U.S. Army Materiel Command (AMC)

The Army **Materiel** Command has the mission of providing the Army with the latest and best military technology available, as well as finding technological solutions to operational problems. It is headquartered in Alexandria, Virginia, and has over 67,000 personnel at its disposal.

U.S. Army Training and Doctrine Command (TRADOC)

TRADOC takes responsibility for training U.S. Army personnel. It contains 27 military schools and 9,167 instructors. In 2000 alone, TRADOC trained over 316,000 military personnel, including 268,800 soldiers and 3,760 foreign soldiers.

Eighth U.S. Army (EUSA), Korea

The Eighth U.S. Army is a force of some 26,500 personnel stationed in the Republic of South Korea. Its purpose is to protect South Korea from possible communist threats from North Korea and also to give the U.S. Army a vital base within the troubled southeast Asia region.

U.S. Army Corps of Engineers (USACE)

The USACE actually consists of approximately 34,600 civilians and only 650 military personnel. Its mission is to support the United States at home and abroad with vital engineering projects. These projects include establishing water supplies, constructing military facilities and bases, supporting other federal and defense agencies with development projects, and providing engineering response in case of national emergencies and disasters. USACE is headquartered in Washington, D.C.

U.S. Army Medical Command (MEDCOM)

MEDCOM incorporates the Army's hospital and dental facilities, developing health programs and training combat medical personnel. It even has a veterinary command for the care of animals in military service. Each day, MEDCOM facilities receive over 37,000 clinic visits and carry out 41,400 dental procedures.

U.S. Army Pacific Command (USARPAC)

Formed in 1957, USARPAC contributes toward stability in the Pacific region and has strategic relations with over 41 countries,

A soldier of the 8th U.S. Army keeps watch over the border territories between U.S.-protected South Korea and communist North Korea. U.S. troop commitment in Korea is currently around 36,000 personnel.

ARMY NATIONAL GUARD

The National Guard is a reserve element of the U.S. Army. It is manned mainly by civilians who act as soldiers on a part-time basis. Typical service involves the individual contributing one weekend each month and a two-week period of extended training in the summer. The National Guard fulfills both state and federal roles. The governor of a state can call upon the National Guard to assist with state emergencies, such as natural disasters, riots, or breakdowns in social order. In a federal capacity, the National Guard is used to support regular forces on peacekeeping, humanitarian, and military operations at home and abroad. The National Guard has served in recent conflicts, such as the Gulf War, and is currently being used to provide domestic protection in the war against terrorism.

including the Philippines, Thailand, Vietnam, Japan, Mongolia, Russia, China, South Korea, India, Bangladesh, Australia, New Zealand, Marshall Islands, and Papua New Guinea. Current numbers of personnel deployed are around 38,000.

U.S. Army Space and Missile Defense Command (SMDC)

The SMDC is the U.S. Army's newest Military Command, created on October 1, 1997. It implements the Army's space and national missile-defense policies, providing defense against nuclear **ballistic** missile attack and also exploring the development of space-based weapons systems.

Military Traffic Management Command (MTMC)

The MTMC provides national and international transportation services to the Army and other military services. Using shipping alone, it transported over 3.1 million tons of military **logistics** last year, and has 24 dedicated ports of its own around the world.

U.S. Army Military District of Washington (MDW)

The MDW has some 7,500 military personnel on active duty and executes two main roles. First, it protects the nation's capital from aggressors and acts as a disaster-relief agency. Second, it conducts official public and ceremonial events for government and military occasions around the capital.

U.S. Army South (USARSO)

A small force of around 1,800 personnel, USARSO provides support to U.S. embassies and military groups throughout Central and South America and the Caribbean. It frequently conducts humanitarian operations throughout Latin America and is head-quartered in Puerto Rico.

U.S. Army Intelligence and Security Command (INSCOM)

INSCOM conducts surveillance and gathers intelligence to support military planning and operations worldwide. It has units stationed in Germany, Panama, Japan, Korea, the United Kingdom, and Hawaii, but its personnel are found wherever the U.S. Army needs intelligence support. The headquarters of INSCOM are in Fort Belvoir, Virginia.

Here, U.S. Army Special Forces Green Berets are seen training Vietnamese special forces during the Vietnam War, 1967. The weapon is an M79 grenade launcher, affectionately nicknamed the "blooper" by U.S. troops on account of the strange noise it makes when fired.

U.S. Army Criminal Investigation Command (CID)

CID investigates felony violations of the Uniform Code of Military Justice and any significant criminal case pending within or against the Army. It has the full capabilities of any major law enforcement agency, including a criminal records repository, forensic laboratory, procurement fraud unit, and counternarcotics team.

In December 1999, areas of Venezuela were hit by horrific mudslides after torrential rain. The U.S. Army flew in medical teams and helped with the emergency airlifts, rescuing people from remote rural areas. Here, a young girl is carried from a U.S. Army helicopter.

U.S. Army Special Operations Command (USASOC)

USASOC has the overall responsibility for recruiting, training, equipping, and deploying U.S. Army special operations personnel throughout the world. It is a very busy Major Command. During a 10-month period in 1996 and 1997, for example, 23,000 USASOC soldiers deployed to 100 countries and conducted 1,600 missions. Around 10,000 Special Forces troops are trained every year at U.S. Army John F. Kennedy Special Warfare Center and School at Fort Bragg, North Carolina.

THE GREATEST SECURITY FORCE ON EARTH

All these commands build up into the greatest security force on earth, and keep the U.S. Army functioning smoothly. Currently in charge of this force is General Eric K. Shinseki, the U.S. Army Chief of Staff. After graduating from the United States Military Academy in 1965, General Shinseki went on two combat tours as an artillery observer in Vietnam in the 1960s and began an impressive rise through the ranks of the Army.

General Shinseki is said to demonstrate the best of Army qualities: understanding, discipline, compassion, and the ability to get the job done quickly and efficiently. Yet though he occupies the highest rank in the U.S. Army, all Army soldiers are expected to have these same character traits. Every officer and soldier within the U.S. Army commands has been trained to perform specialized and highly demanding duties. What most of them have in common, however, is that they have all gone through the difficulties and challenges of basic training.

TRAINING FOR DEFENSE

All U.S. Army soldiers have to go through Basic Training, eight weeks of arduous physical and mental training. The course is tough, but it ensures that the men and women who emerge at the other end are among the best regular soldiers in the world.

U.S. Army training consists of two stages: Basic Training (BT) and Advanced Individual Training (AIT). BT is the training program that turns new recruits into soldiers, and it is followed by AIT, which turns the soldiers into military specialists. During BT, the much-feared drill sergeants (DSs) will be looking for individuals who can demonstrate character, endurance, and teamwork in the face of physical exhaustion and hard discipline.

BASIC TRAINING

Army training is conducted in any of a number of locations. The particular training school that a new recruit ends up in will usually be related to the location of his AIT. Some of the most popular destinations for BT are Fort Knox in Louisville, Kentucky; Fort Jackson in Columbia, South Carolina; Fort McClellan in Anniston,

Left: A soldier stops and listens during combat training. His rifle has a device that fires harmless laser beams, which enable a soldier to tell whether he has "hit" an opponent.

During Basic Training, U.S. Army recruits have to perform hundreds of push-ups, sit-ups, and other exercises. The recruits are awarded points for performing certain physical exercises, and they have to reach an acceptable points total to move on to the next stage.

Alabama; Fort Leonard Wood in Waynesville, Missouri; and Fort Still in Lawton, Oklahoma.

BT is actually of nine-weeks' duration, but the first week is spent in what is known as the Reception Battalion. The Reception Battalion is the place where the new recruit is processed and made ready for training. This first week is quite tedious for the enthusiastic recruits. They will receive inoculations, have dental examinations, fill out official paperwork and life-insurance forms, receive their ID papers, and get their first regulation Army haircut. There are also some basic intelligence tests and a fitness test. The

HARSHNESS OF THE DRILL INSTRUCTORS

Private First Class Robert Bowles gives insight into life during
Basic Training:

It was common for soldiers to keep the combination on their
locker already dialed in, so all they had to do was pull it open in
the morning, thus saving a few seconds. Evidently, the drill
sergeant had been going around searching for those troops doing
that. And alas, I was the one he found.

"Drill sergeant," I said, "the private was—"

"Didn't I tell you to shut up? Now you're ignoring me! Drop and
give me 40 while I do a locker inspection!"

I dropped to the cold, hard floor and began knocking out the
push-ups as he opened my locker and grabbed my uniforms, shirts,
socks, underwear, and towels and threw them down the middle of
the barracks. By the time I was done with my push-ups, and had
recovered to the position of attention, my locker was empty. He
warned me that if I ever left one of his lockers unsecured again, he
was going to throw me down the barracks aisle.

fitness test includes 15 push-ups, 17 sit-ups, and a 0.5-mile (0.8-
km) run (to be completed in 8.5 minutes); the test varies slightly,
according to the drill sergeant and the gender of the recruit.

Once the Reception Battalion period is over, the recruits can look
forward to the eight weeks of BT proper. BT is broken down into
three phases: Phase I, known as "Red Phase"; Phase II, "White
Phase"; and Phase III, "Blue Phase."

A soldier training to enter the U.S. Army Rangers tackles an obstacle course. The initial Ranger physical fitness test for new recruits includes 49 push-ups, 59 sit-ups, and a two-mile run in 15 minutes or less.

PHASE I—RED PHASE

Phase I runs from Week 1 to Week 3 of BT. Week 1 is a great shock for the recruits. They are introduced to their fearsome drill sergeant, a scowling, seemingly humorless individual who picks up on every offense against discipline, no matter how small. The recruits have to follow the drill sergeant's commands to the letter, and the typical day lasts from 4.30 A.M. to 9:00 P.M. They learn how to make beds the Army way, wear their uniforms properly, clean their **barracks** and lockers, maintain their rifle and equipment, and identify the

A Ranger recruit crawls through the dust. The initial phase of Ranger training takes place at Fort Benning, Georgia. This phase tests the recruit's physical fitness and combat skills. The program is so demanding that over 60 percent can fail to make the grade.

various military ranks of the Army. Physical training also begins in earnest: lots of running (a common distance is 2 miles [3.2 km]), push-ups, sit-ups, and assault courses.

Week 2 continues the training. An inspection is made of the recruits' living space, locker, rifle, and equipment. Every fault receives a sharp reprimand or punishment. The trainees will receive instruction in parade-ground drill and ceremonies, but they will also have their first combat training, learning some of the basics of

Live firing is a vital element of Army training. Only by using live ammunition will recruits become accustomed to the sensations of real battle. Here, two Army soldiers prepare to fire into a section of woodland with an M16A2 rifle (left) and an M60 machine-gun.

U.S. ARMY CORE VALUES

Loyalty—Bear true faith and allegiance to the U.S. Constitution, the Army, your unit, and other soldiers

Duty—Fulfill your obligations

Respect—Treat people as they should be treated

Selfless Service—Put the welfare of the nation, the Army, and your subordinates before your own

Honor—Live up to all the Army values

Integrity—Do what is right, legally and morally

Personal Courage—Face fear, danger, or adversity (physical or moral)

bayonet fighting and combat first aid. They have a detailed introduction to their gun, the M16A2 rifle.

A distinctive exercise of Week 2 (sometimes Week 3) is the "Gas Chamber." This is a room filled with **CS gas**. Each recruit has to step inside, then twice remove his respirator to recount his name, rank, and social security number. Most recruits emerge with eyes stinging and full of tears; many are also vomiting.

Week 3 builds up the physical exercise and combat training and includes sparring with pugil sticks, unarmed combat training and land navigation instruction.

PHASE II—WHITE PHASE

White Phase lasts for Weeks 4–6. Week 4 takes the recruits to the firing ranges, where they learn to use the M16A2 rifle, shooting at a

variety of moving, pop-up, and long-range targets. Soon, they progress to hand grenades. At first, only dummy grenades are thrown, then each recruit gets to throw fragmentation grenades.

Week 5 increases the demands of M16 marksmanship, and the recruit will practice automatic fire and night firing. The recruit needs to hit at least 17 out of 40 targets to pass as a "marksman," but a strike rate of more than 24 will earn a "sharpshooter" badge. Physical training focuses on combat-type assault courses. The recruits have to run around the obstacle course in full **kit**. Live machine-gun fire will sometimes be directed over their heads, or small **pyrotechnics** charges will be detonated nearby to increase the impression of combat. To compensate for this trauma, the recruits will then be introduced to firing light antitank weapons, like the LAW rocket.

Week 6 raises the physical demands. In full kit, they will have to negotiate eight-mile (13-km) speed-marches and perform well in the many physical exercises. At this stage, many recruits notice that they are starting to think, behave, and perform more like soldiers. Whether this is actually true or not is tested in Phase III.

PHASE III—BLUE PHASE

Blue Phase tests the military skills and physical strength that the recruits should have picked up over the previous six weeks. During

Left: U.S. Army recruits are taught the principles of camouflage, concealment, and decoy (CCD) to increase their survivability on the battlefield. Here, a soldier digs a foxhole. If he has time to prepare, he should dig a hole that is shoulder-deep when standing up.

Week 7, the recruits take their final PT test, the Standard Army Annual PT exam. They must score at least 150 points to pass this, but by this stage, most do so without too much trouble.

After this, the recruits embark on a one-week period of full-blown military exercises, which include digging foxholes, deploying ambushes and patrols, and showing their abilities to communicate effectively and respond to crises. If they can come through this end-of-cycle test, they will be classified as U.S. Army soldiers. After spending most of Week 8 in preparation, they will then attend a formal graduation ceremony.

ADVANCED INDIVIDUAL TRAINING AND OFFICER TRAINING

AIT is an extension of BT and teaches soldiers their Military Occupational Specialty (MOS). The MOS training programs vary greatly, depending on what profession the soldier pursues within the Army—there are over 400 different types of jobs within the U.S. armed forces for a soldier to do. A soldier could go on to become a tank gunner, airborne soldier, helicopter pilot, artillery gunner, or intelligence operative. Often, the AIT is conducted at the same place as the BT, and the typical soldier may undergo about 13 weeks of training from the beginning of the BT to the end of the AIT.

Officers are recruited into the Army from several sources, chiefly the Reserve Officer Training Corps (ROTC) at various universities and colleges throughout the United States; the Officer Candidate School at Fort Benning, Georgia; and prestigious institutions, like

A group of U.S. Army officers practice negotiating a river in an inflatable dinghy. Depending on the branch of the Army, officer training can take up to a year. Even after that, there may be more training as the officer learns a particular military specialty.

the U.S. Military Academy at West Point. Standard training to be a U.S. Army officer can last up to a year. In institutions like West Point, where the cadets also take baccalaureate degrees over a four-year course, only 1,300 soldiers pass out of about 14,000 applicants each year. Officers undergo the same BT as regular soldiers, although they often have to show more advanced physical fitness. They also have to demonstrate the qualities of leadership and character necessary to inspire soldiers in battle.

Whether training officers or regular soldiers, the U.S. Army consistently produces superb troops well-versed in the arts of war.

WEAPONS OF THE U.S. ARMY

No other army in the world comes close to the power of the U.S. Army's weapons systems. The U.S. defense industry has kept the Army at the cutting edge of military technology, knowing that the future defense of the United States depends on it.

On February 4, 1991, during the Gulf War (1990–1991), the Allied forces launched a massive assault from Saudi Arabia into neighboring Kuwait and Iraq. Their goal was to push the occupying Iraqi forces out of Kuwait and back into Iraq. They faced nearly half a million Iraqi troops and a massive force of enemy tanks, mainly Soviet-era T-62s and T-72s. The T-72, in particular, was well able to destroy a tank at distances of over two miles (3.2 km) with its advanced anti-armor ammunition. However, they were up against nearly 1,900 U.S. Army M1A1 Abrams tanks, the most advanced tank in the world.

When the tank armies finally clashed, the Iraqis were totally outclassed. The Abrams is capable of firing accurately even while on the move over rough ground, and its advanced 120-mm smooth-bore Rheinmetall gun outranged the Iraqi firepower by over 3,048 feet

Left: The Patriot is the most advanced surface-to-air missile system in the world. When launched, its missiles reach supersonic speeds within only 20 ft (6.6 m) of leaving the launcher.

(1,000 m). Using Forward-Looking InfraRed (FLIR) technology, the crews could also see all the Iraqi vehicles, even in the darkness of night or through the smoke and dust of desert battle. In total, the Iraqis lost 3,847 tanks during the war; no U.S. tanks were lost to Iraqi armor.

This battle illustrates why technology can be decisive in conflict. The U.S. Army spends over $30 billion each year on developing new equipment for waging war. It would be impossible to list the many different types of weaponry in the U.S. arsenal, but we can look at some of the individual weapons that contribute to the Army's technological superiority on any battlefield.

M1A2 ABRAMS MAIN BATTLE TANK

We have already seen the capabilities of the M1A1 Abrams tank. The latest U.S. tank is the M1A2 upgrade of the Abrams, and it represents the best of worldwide tank technology. The basic M1 Abrams tank has a weight of 120,249 lb (54,545 kg) and a maximum road speed of 44 mph (72km/h). It is armed with one 105-mm main gun, two 7.62-mm machine guns, one .50-caliber machine gun, and six smoke-grenade launchers. It has day and night fire-on-the-move capability; a laser range finder, to give the precise distance to a target; a thermal-imaging night sight; optical day sight; and a digital ballistic computer, to calculate the precise targeting of the gun, allowing for wind, distance, and the movement of the enemy vehicle. Its armor type is classified, but it can stop most anti-tank shells. The Abrams can also be fitted with explosive reactive armor. This armor has an explosive filling that, when struck by an

An M1 Abrams tank plows its way across the desert landscape in the Gulf War. The U.S. Army did not lose a single tank to enemy armored vehicles, and the Iraqi army was completely outclassed by the superior technology of weapons such as the M1.

enemy shell, explodes outward and thus cancels the force of the explosion against it.

The basic M1 is a superb machine, but it is far surpassed by the M1A2. The M1A2 has a new FLIR targeting system for its 120-mm gun, which has given a 70 percent improvement in finding the target, 45 percent improvement in the speed of fire, a 30 percent greater range, and enhanced accuracy. A Thermal Management System (TMS) keeps the temperature inside the tank always below 95°F (35°C), whatever the combat conditions. Although other nations have advanced tanks, such as the British Challenger II and

In 1991, perhaps the worst place in the world to be was inside an Iraqi army tank. While U.S. Army Apache helicopters and U.S. Air Force jets destroyed enemy vehicles from the air, U.S. and allied tanks devastated them on the ground. Here is a destroyed Iraqi T-55 vehicle, an outdated Soviet tank.

French Le Clerc, the M1A2 Abrams is recognized as being the best tank in the world today.

AH-64 APACHE

The U.S. Army has a large fleet of aircraft, both fixed-wing (airplanes) and rotary-wing (helicopters). Its fixed-wing fleet is largely concerned with transportation and uses aircraft such as the C-130 Hercules and C-23 Sherpa. However, it is the rotary-wing aircraft that have now become the most influential combat aircraft in the U.S. Army. The Army created the concept of the helicopter gunship back in the Vietnam conflict, and several decades later, it has produced the ultimate war machine, the AH-64 Apache.

The Apache entered service in 1984, having been developed by McDonnell Douglas (now Boeing). More than 800 Apaches are currently in service with the Army. They were used to great effect during the Gulf War, when entire Iraqi columns of armored vehicles were destroyed by Apaches hovering many miles away, out of visual range, but within weapons range.

The Apache is a twin-engined attack helicopter. Its firepower is awesome. It carries a 30-mm Boeing M230 chain gun under its nose, which is capable of firing 625 explosive cannon shells per minute. Anti-armor capability is provided by 16 Lockheed Martin/Boeing AGM-114D Longbow Hellfire air-to-surface missiles. These have a maximum range of 7.4 miles (12 km) and work in "fire-and-forget" mode—in other words, they guide themselves to the target once released without the assistance of the helicopter crew. Using the millimeter-wave Longbow seeker radar, the Hellfires can be launched even though the crew cannot see their target. From spotting a target to launching a missile can take as little as 30 seconds, and its onboard computers can track, monitor, and target up to 265 separate targets at once. Other weapons include four Sidewinder air-to-air missiles for defense against enemy aircraft; and pods of 2.75-inch rockets for use against area targets. All information derived from the target-acquisition system is visually presented in the monocular eyepiece of the Honeywell-integrated Helmet And Display Sighting System

(HADDS) worn by the pilot and copilot. Apaches will remain at the vanguard of U.S. Army operations for the foreseeable future, and over 1,000 have been exported to countries abroad who want to benefit from the Apache's amazing versatility and firepower.

MULTIPLE LAUNCH ROCKET SYSTEM (MLRS)

While the U.S. Army has many fine artillery pieces in its arsenal, the single most-devastating is the MLRS M270. This is not a gun, but a mobile rocket-launcher system. The launcher vehicle carries 12 rocket tubes. The tubes can be loaded and fired in a ripple pattern in

APACHE MISSION

Lieutenant Colonel William Bryan, 2nd Battalion/229th Aviation Regiment, describes the experience of using an Apache helicopter against an Iraqi column during the Gulf War:

"There were hundreds of vehicles in the column. This time, we were fired on; we were engaged by several heat-seeking missiles, and we think some radar-guided SAM-6s were fired. It was like an inferno; there was so much smoke that none of the enemy systems could acquire us. Most of what we fired at we hit, however. Visually, you could see the flash of the explosions going off in the tunnel-like darkness, but through the FLIR, the intense heat created by burning vehicles was easily visible.... It all happened very quickly. At the same time, you are so focused and keyed up that it seemed to take forever for the Hellfire to get to the target, although it was only a couple of seconds."

This view of an Apache helicopter shows its superb technology and weaponry. Eight Hellfire antitank missiles are mounted on each side of the fuselage. The dome on the top of the aircraft is its advanced radar system. Just beneath the cockpit is a powerful surveillance camera and multibarrel machine-gun.

The Multiple Launch Rocket System (MLRS) is a terrifying weapon. Using rockets with multiple warheads, it can deliver nearly 8,000 explosive devices in less than 60 seconds and at ranges of over 20 miles (32 km). The MLRS is in service with 15 nations.

only five minutes, and each high-explosive or cluster-bomb rocket has a range of up to 31 miles (50 km), although the Army TACMS Block IA missile can reach up to 186 miles (300 km). The effect on the target is devastating. One Iraqi officer in the Gulf War told how his unit was reduced from 600 men to only 175 after a single strike by the MLRS. Each rocket can be programmed to explode just above the ground, so that the enemy has little chance to find shelter, and M77 warheads split into 644 small, individual bombs that either explode immediately or detonate some time later. Another warhead, the AT2, disperses 28 antitank mines over the target area.

The latest MLRS features an Improved Fire Control System (IFCS), which uses the Global Positioning System (GPS) to put down rockets within a few yards of the target.

FUTURE WARRIORS

The Abrams tank, the Apache, and the MLRS are just three examples of the war-winning technologies that protect the United States. There are many more. The individual soldier in the U.S. Army has never been better armed, and there is no army on earth that comes close to matching U.S. Army firepower.

So what of the future? One of the most important developments for the individual soldier is the Land Warrior Project, due to come to fruition in 2004. Land Warrior is a 16.6-lb (7.5-kg) portable laptop computer built into the soldier's uniform. The computer is linked up to a Head-Mounted Display (HMD) **monocle** worn over the left eye, through which the soldier sees a digitized plan of the battlefield and receives a stream of tactical information, including the geophysical contours ahead, the position of all unit members, the position of enemy forces, enemy weaponry information, large-scale maps of the area, the soldier's location via GPS, and logistics information.

The computer console is worn on the chest with a flip-down screen, the mouse being located on the soldier's rifle, and can be used silently to send e-mails and operational data between soldiers and backup forces. To improve efficiency, laser sensors and thermal-imaging systems on the rifle—which are connected to the computer—enable the soldier to target an enemy accurately at night

OBJECTIVE INDIVIDUAL COMBAT WEAPON

At present, the U.S. Army uses the M16A2 rifle as its standard infantry firearm. However, over the next 10 years, more and more M16s are likely to be replaced by the Objective Individual Combat Weapon (OICW). The OICW is the ultimate in futuristic firepower. It has two main weapons: a 0.21-in (5.56-mm) assault rifle and a 0.5-in (20-mm) grenade launcher. Both weapons use a computerized infrared electronic aiming system, which allows targeting even at night and through smoke. The grenade launcher is also fitted with a laser range-finder. This fires out a laser beam that tells the ammunition in the weapon the exact distance to the target. When the grenade is fired, it is programmed to explode in the air directly above the target. Even an enemy hiding behind a wall is not safe from such a weapon.

or in zero visibility, and even to aim the weapon around corners without breaking cover at all.

Land Warrior is a glimpse into the future of war, but it is a future that will come soon. The U.S. Army will work hard to make sure that its technology is always the best possible to help its soldiers survive battles and to quash the tactics of any enemy.

Right: The M16A1 (pictured) and the M16A2 are the standard rifles of the U.S. Army. The M16A2 differs from the M16A1 in that it has a three-round burst facility—pull the trigger once and three bullets are fired—as an option apart from the standard single-shot setting.

CHEMICAL, NUCLEAR, AND BIOLOGICAL DEFENSE

The attacks of September 11, 2001, and the subsequent anthrax attacks via the U.S. mail system awoke America to the possible threats from what are known as weapons of mass destruction (WMD).

WMD are chemical, biological, or nuclear devices that are capable of killing over 5,000 people in a single deployment. Though the **anthrax** attacks did not achieve a large death toll, the disruption to daily life was enormous. Fortunately, however, the U.S. Army is prepared to meet the challenge of further WMD attacks with two of its own special departments: the U.S. Army Space and Missile Defense Command (SMDC) and the U.S. Army Soldier and Biological Chemical Command (SBCCOM).

U.S. ARMY SPACE AND MISSILE DEFENSE COMMAND (SMDC)

Although the United States has played its part in reducing the amount of nuclear weapons in the world, many more countries have acquired nuclear capabilities over the last 20 years. China now has

Left: A soldier in the Gulf War (1990–1991) wears protective clothing. Iraq had previously used lethal chemical agents against its own people, so U.S. forces deployed chemical and biological warfare units.

CHEMICAL, NUCLEAR, AND BIOLOGICAL DEFENSE 61

the Dong Feng series of Intercontinental Ballistic Missiles (ICBMs), including the Dong Feng 31. This can deliver a single 2.5-megaton nuclear warhead (equivalent to 2.5 millions tons of dynamite being exploded) or three 90-kiloton (90,000 tons of dynamite) up to a range of 7,500 miles (12,065 km)—far enough to reach the United States. China is not the only country to develop nuclear capabilities. Both India and Pakistan, traditionally great enemies of each other, have nuclear arsenals. Iraq is believed to be attempting to develop nuclear weapons. Communist North Korea has also been developing a nuclear arsenal since 1947.

SMDC is the part of the U.S. Army that combats this nuclear threat. It is a Major Command and focuses on exploiting space for military purposes and producing the technology to protect the United States from nuclear attack. SMDC is the newest of the Major Commands, created on October 1, 1997. However, the Army has been responsible for ballistic missile defense since the 1950s. In 1962, the Army used a Nike-Zeus missile to successfully intercept a test ballistic missile during its flight.

Today, SMDC has a sophisticated range of earthbound and space-based technologies either ready for action or in development. Three in particular are worth mentioning: the Patriot Advanced Capability 3 (PAC-3), the Theater High Altitude Area Defense (THAAD), and the Space-Based Laser (SBL).

Left: Patriot missile systems were used to intercept enemy ballistic missiles during the Gulf War. Patriot batteries managed to destroy several Iraqi Scud missiles fired at Israel.

The PAC-3 is a high-velocity, surface-to-air missile that can hit incoming ballistic missiles and destroy their high-explosive, biological, chemical, or nuclear warheads. It actively seeks out the enemy missile, climbing to an altitude of 78,750 feet (24,000 m) in a matter of seconds before exploding in the attacking missile's vicinity. It has a range of 37 miles (60 km). Patriots were used in action in the Gulf War to down Iraqi **Scud** missiles fired at Israel. Since then, major improvements have been made to increase their accuracy, speed, and knock-down power. Patriots are often part of the THAAD system.

THAAD consists of the rocket launcher, plus the THAAD radar system and the THAAD battle management/command, control, communications, and intelligence (BM/C3I) system. The THAAD's radar technology tracks all incoming missiles, then targets them and releases a Patriot or similar missile in seconds, tracking the missile to target while it is in flight. The full THAAD system should be operational by 2004.

The SBL is the future of the Army's missile-defense program. Special combat satellites will orbit the Earth armed with high-powered laser beams. The satellites will be able to detect any ballistic missile at the very moment it is launched—wherever on the globe it is launched from—then track it and attack it with lasers until the missile is destroyed. Current plans hope to see the SBL tested in 2012 and operational shortly thereafter. With a network of such weapons orbiting the Earth, the U.S. Army could provide an almost impenetrable shield of protection over the United States against missile attacks.

The U.S. military has early-warning stations across the globe—this one is stationed in the polar region. Stations such as this monitor the Earth constantly for signs of hostile missile launches.

U.S. ARMY SOLDIER AND BIOLOGICAL CHEMICAL COMMAND (SBCOM)

Chemical and biological weapons are some of the most frightening WMDs. Several countries hostile to the United States have biological and chemical warfare. Iraq, for instance, has the lethal agents anthrax, botulinum toxin, ricin, and aflatoxin, and is also developing at least 34 other agents for use in warfare.

SBCOM's role is to guard the United States against these threats. Its mission states: "Develop, integrate, acquire, and sustain soldier and NBC defense technology, systems, and services to ensure the decisive edge and maximum protection for the United States." In addition to developing or disposing of chemical and biological weapons, SBCOM is involved with preparing the U.S. Army to deal effectively with any WMD attack within U.S. shores. It has its own rapid-response force—the Army Technical Escort Unit. This highly trained chemical/biological response team has over 50 years of experience in handling chemical and biological threats and materials.

SBCOM has a vital role in preparing U.S. soldiers for chemical and biological warfare, developing the protective suits, detection tools, and decontamination equipment that will enable the Army to keep functioning in even the most hostile C&B environment. It is also involved in the federal Domestic Preparedness Program (DPP). The DPP sends SBCOM personnel out into U.S. communities, and trains local civilian, emergency, and law enforcement agencies in dealing with chemical and biological incidents. Over 105 communities have received special training.

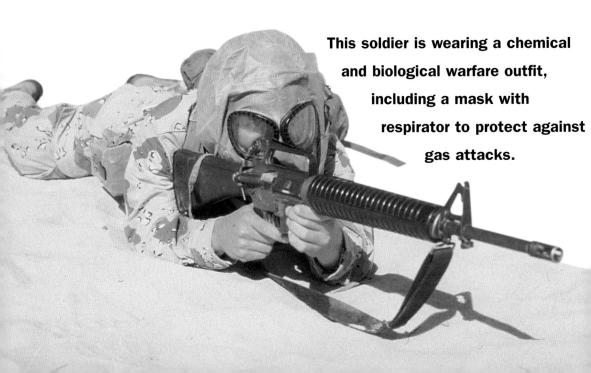

This soldier is wearing a chemical and biological warfare outfit, including a mask with respirator to protect against gas attacks.

DANGERS FROM ANTHRAX

Following the September 11, 2001 attacks on America, the U.S. suffered a series of biological attacks using the bacteria anthrax. Anthrax is the disease produced by the bacteria Bacillus anthracis.

The U.S. Army has an elite force trained to deal with WMD threats. Here personnel are wearing full biological warfare outfits.

It is a lethal disease and one particularly useful for terrorist use since it is easy to manufacture, can be spread over a wide area, and can be stored for a long time. There are three types of anthrax: cutaneous anthrax—infection through the skin or via a cut; gastrointestinal anthrax—infection through eating anthrax-contaminated foods; and inhalation anthrax—infection through breathing in anthrax spores. The last type is by far the most dangerous. The symptoms begin with a flu-like illness followed by severe difficulty in breathing, internal bleeding, and ultimately, respiratory collapse. Thankfully, there were few deaths from inhalation anthrax following the 2001 attacks, and U.S. Army and civilian disease-control scientists are already developing antidotes and vaccines to combat this terrible threat.

FIGHTING FOR FREEDOM ABROAD

The U.S. Army is not only committed to homeland defense. As part of the United States' ongoing attempts to make the world more peaceable and democratic, the Army is constantly deployed across the world in the causes of freedom and humanitarian aid.

Since World War II, the roles of the U.S. Army have changed tremendously. It still has its traditional duty of fighting, of course: during the last 50 years, the Army has fought in major wars, including the Korean War (1950–1952), the Vietnam War (1963–1975), the Gulf War (1990–1991), and, at present, the war against terrorism in Afghanistan (2001–). Yet this type of operation is only part of what the Army accomplishes; its work also includes what are known as operations other than war (OOTW). OOTW include delivering humanitarian relief, acting as peacekeeping troops in foreign war zones, providing engineering support in poor countries, combating drug trafficking, and apprehending foreign warlords.

This demanding breadth of operations takes the U.S. Army all over the world; the soldiers trying also to promote social

Left: With their M3-A2 Bradley Armored Fighting Vehicle parked nearby, two U.S. Army soldiers make a communications stop during a patrol in Bosnia-Herzegovir Europe. The soldiers were part of the UN peacekeeping operation, Operation Joint Endeavor.

harmony and democratic values. For example, in Africa alone, the U.S. Army is performing the following tasks:

U.S. Army explosive-**ordnance** disposal experts have been deployed to Nigeria, central Africa, to help local military forces clear away unexploded bombs and mines left over from its civil war.

Soldiers from the U.S. Army Corps of Engineers are helping to build flood defenses in the countries of Mozambique, Botswana, South Africa, and Zimbabwe as part of Operation Atlas Response.

U.S. Army troops have built a 430,520-square foot (40,000-sq-m)

Iraqi prisoners are searched after the massive defeat of the Iraqi army during the Gulf War. Although they were the former enemy of the U.S. forces, all prisoners were given humanitarian treatment. Many even asked if they could become U.S. citizens after the war.

aid center in Gabon, which will be used to store aid materials and can also house refugees in times of disaster. As part of the African Crisis Response Initiative, U.S. Army soldiers train African troops in the techniques of humanitarian and peacekeeping work, including convoy protection, food distribution, and the treating of refugees. Similar work is being conducted around the world in regions such as southern Europe, Latin America, and the Far East, as well as homeland U.S. territories. These operations often go unreported by the world's media.

OOTW form a large part of the U.S. Army's worldwide commitment. Unfortunately, however, operations involving combat are all-too-regular. Many U.S. soldiers have sacrificed their lives in action since World War II, defending against tyranny and oppression in various forms. Between 1950 and 1952, the U.S. Army formed a large part of the United Nations army fighting Communist North Korea, which was attempting to take over democratic South Korea. Similarly, U.S. ground troops in 1963–1973 fought in the defense of South Vietnam against Communist North Vietnam in the Vietnam War. The Gulf War was concerned with ejecting Iraqi forces from their occupation of neighboring Kuwait. U.S. forces in the former Yugoslavia, Europe, were deployed in the 1990s to prevent the massacre and displacement of millions of local people. In all these cases, the United States Army was sent to defend peoples whom the world could well have abandoned to their fate.

We will now look at two of the landmark operations of the last 30 years, both involving the U.S. Army's elite Rangers, and we will see what lessons the Army has learned.

The Vietnam War was a low point for the U.S. Army. The war was not popular, soldiers were disillusioned, and some troops faced combat almost every single day. After Vietnam, the U.S. was much more cautious about becoming involved in other countries' wars.

Education is a vital part of U.S. Army missions overseas. Here, an Army translator explains to children in the war-torn country of Bosnia-Herzegovina the dangers of antipersonnel mines and unexploded bombs. The intention is to reduce the number of deaths among children caused by military weapons.

GRENADA, 1983

On October 19, 1983, the government of Grenada (an island in the Caribbean) was overthrown in a bloody act of revolution. The new government was hard-line Communist, and the safety of over 1,000 U.S. medical students and their families on the island was in jeopardy. The Organization of Eastern Caribbean States requested that the United States make a military intervention, and the U.S. government quickly agreed.

A soldier on the Caribbean island of Grenada delivers some basic first aid to a local. The U.S. invasion of Grenada led to the rescue of over 1,000 U.S. medical students and their families, and was one of the biggest U.S. Army operations of the 1980s.

Time was of the essence. A large U.S. Army, Navy, and Air Force operation was quickly put together and launched on October 25. The key to the operation, named Operation Urgent Fury, was the swift capture of the Port Salinas airfield, thus enabling U.S. troops to be landed and from there advance to the True Blue Medical Campus to rescue the U.S. citizens, and then to gain further security by capturing the Cuban army camp at Calivigny. U.S. Army Rangers prepared for dramatic action. They planned to launch their action from C-130 aircraft, which were to land on the airstrip.

A TRIBUTE

Richard Menezes, witness to the action during Operation Urgent Fury, pays tribute to a U.S. soldier, Captain Keith Lucas, killed in the hostilities:

"I live in Grenada and was 11 years old when Operation Urgent Fury took place. I thank God every day for the U.S. intervention and for ex-President Ronald Reagan's decision. It was such a long time ago when it happened, but the name Lucas cannot be forgotten. This brave soldier lost his life in battle, not too far from my house in the south of the island.... I also had the pleasure of meeting his father when he came to Grenada some time after. This soldier died fighting in my country, which I can say today because of brave soldiers like Mr. Lucas.

"May God rest his soul...."

Richard Menezes

However, when the operation was launched, it was found that the airstrip had been covered in obstacles. Within 15 minutes, the Rangers had prepared themselves for a parachute jump.

At 6.30 A.M., the Rangers began their jump. They immediately met resistance, but by 10 A.M., the Rangers had quashed enemy fire and cleared the runway for reinforcements and equipment to be flown in. The Rangers quickly advanced to the True Blue Campus, and the U.S. students were taken unharmed to the airfield, from where they were evacuated. The only disaster of the operation occurred when three Black Hawk helicopters crashed during the assault on the Calivigny army base, in which three Rangers died.

Despite Operation Urgent Fury revealing several problems in U.S. military operations, it had been a success. All U.S. citizens were rescued from the island, and total U.S. casualties were 19 dead and 152 wounded. The Rangers, in particular, had demonstrated their capability as one of the U.S. Army's top units.

MOGADISHU, SOMALIA, 1993

The battle in Mogadishu—capital of the African country Somalia—took place in October 1993, and has gone down in history as one of the most dramatic U.S. Army actions since World War II. It was recently immortalized in the Hollywood movie *Black Hawk Down*.

In 1993, U.S. Army troops were stationed in Somalia, performing humanitarian roles. The troops of a local warlord, Mohammed Farah Aidid, were responsible for much of the continuing violence around the capital, Mogadishu. It was eventually decided that Aidid had to be removed to stabilize the situation. At 3.30 P.M. on October 3, 1993, a flight of U.S. Black Hawk helicopters took off, carrying a large assault team of U.S. Rangers and Delta Force operatives. They were heading for the Olympic Hotel in the center of Mogadishu, where Aidid was supposed to be meeting his lieutenants. The mission was to launch a surprise assault against the hotel, capture Aidid, and bring him to justice.

From the first moment that U.S. troops touched down, however, nothing went according to plan. Hundreds of civilians, all armed with Kalashnikov rifles and rocket-propelled grenades, started firing

U.S. Rangers embark on a patrol in Mogadishu, the capital of Somalia, Africa. Although the Rangers were better armed and better trained than their opponents in 1993, they were totally outnumbered. It is estimated that the Rangers killed over 1,000 Somali gunmen, losing 18 of their own men in the process.

at the Ranger team. While the Rangers established a perimeter around the hotel, the Delta team went inside, but found no Aidid. They did take 20 prisoners, who were loaded onto a convoy of U.S. Army vehicles that had followed the air units into the city. From this moment on, it seemed like all hell had broken loose.

An injured U.S. Ranger is evacuated by a Black Hawk helicopter in Somalia. The Mogadishu firefight began when a Black Hawk helicopter was shot down by a rocket-propelled grenade (RPG).

At 4.20 P.M, a Black Hawk helicopter was shot down by a rocket-propelled grenade five blocks from the hotel. A Ranger unit set off to rescue the crew, but came under blistering fire all the way. Every doorway and window seemed to hold an enemy weapon spraying fire. Even women and children were armed with Kalashnikovs. At 4.40 P.M., another Black Hawk was downed, and two Delta Force soldiers died trying to save the copilot. The convoy with the prisoners attempted to get back to base, but was hindered by a terrifying wall of bullets and rockets. Eventually, it escaped, but 90 Rangers were left behind in the hostile city.

Darkness fell. The Rangers inside Mogadishu fought throughout the night and set up a medical treatment center to treat the many wounded. Little Bird helicopters dropped fresh ammunition and attacked the Somali gunmen, but the situation became increasingly desperate. Back at the base, General Montgomery, the commander of the mission, sent out a rescue convoy. It was beaten back by heavy fire in the narrow streets. Eventually, local Malaysian and Pakistani UN forces lent the U.S. convoy some tanks, and a 70-vehicle fighting convoy eventually broke through to the beleaguered Rangers. At 5.20 A.M. on October 4, the trapped Rangers and the surviving helicopter crew were loaded aboard the convoy. The vehicles were so full that some Rangers had to run out of the city alongside the convoy while under streams of enemy fire. Finally, they made it back to their base in a sports stadium.

Eighteen U.S. soldiers died and 84 were wounded in Mogadishu. The operation had taught the U.S. Army in the harshest possible fashion about the dangers of humanitarian work in dangerous lands. Since Mogadishu, the U.S. Army has been more cautious about the situations into which it sends its soldiers. Yet humanitarian work around the world continues, and the bravery of the soldiers who fought in the battle is an inspiration to all U.S. Army personnel. Two soldiers killed in the fighting received the Congressional Medal of Honor, the highest military decoration in the United States.

Grenada and Mogadishu both demonstrate that U.S. soldiers abroad frequently risk their lives for the health, freedom, and peace of others. They are also engaged in defending the United States against the tyranny of terrorism, the subject of the next chapter.

THE WAR AGAINST TERRORISM

Since September 11, 2001, the United States has been fighting a new war—a war against terrorism. The U.S. Army has put all its resources into this fight, and is already beginning to smash global terrorist organizations using its elite troops.

On September 11, 2001, at 8.45 A.M., American Airlines Flight 11, carrying 81 passengers and 11 crew, smashed into the north tower of the World Trade Center in New York City. Twenty minutes later, United Airlines Flight 175, with 56 passengers and nine crew, hit the south tower. Both towers eventually collapsed from the devastation of the subsequent fire. Approximately half an hour after the second crash, American Airlines Flight 77 took off from Dulles International Airport (outside Washington, D.C.), bound for Los Angeles. Shortly after takeoff, it plowed into the Pentagon building. Thirty minutes later, United Flight 93, from Newark, New Jersey, to San Francisco, crashed near Shanksville, Pennsylvania, killing all 38 passengers and seven crew. The combined death toll from all these incidents exceeded 3,000 people. While the first crash

Left: Soldiers from the 101st Airborne Division watch vigilantly for the enemy during Operation Anaconda, Afghanistan, March 5, 2002. The operation was intended to destroy enemy units hiding out in the Afghan mountains, and resulted in heavy fighting and loss of life on both sides.

seemed like a nightmarish accident, the subsequent crashes soon made it clear that the United States was under a terrorist attack of unimaginable proportions. The country has changed irrevocably since the attacks. No longer can it believe itself immune from world terrorism. While the rest of the world has been experiencing terrorist attacks since the 1950s, the United States has been mainly free from such incidents.

President George W. Bush quickly rose to the challenge of the new situation and declared a "war on terrorism," promising that any terrorist group around the world would be flushed out and destroyed. The U.S. Army has been at the vanguard of this fight, particularly through the use of its special forces, which are uniquely trained to combat terrorists and **insurgents**. The prime suspect for the attacks is the Al Qaeda network, a radical Islamic organization with units, bases, and operatives throughout the Middle East, but particularly concentrated in Afghanistan.

Afghanistan was the base of Al Qaeda's leader, Osama bin Laden, who was seen on video after the attacks, boasting about his planning of them. Previously, in February 1998, he had said that it was the duty of all Muslims to kill U.S. citizens. Sadly, some believed him.

Al Qaeda were protected in Afghanistan by a regime known as the Taliban. The Taliban were a merciless and cruel leadership; under their harsh interpretation of Islamic law, women were beaten for even showing their faces. Afghanistan is one of the poorest countries on earth, and the Taliban made the lives of already desperate people even worse. It was evident in the United States that the fight against terrorism meant overthrowing the Taliban, finding and capturing or

A view of the damage inflicted on the Pentagon after a hijacked American Airlines flight smashed into it on September 11, 2001. Though the damage was severe, it did not hinder a swift U.S. military response to the attacks. Within a month, the U.S. Army was conducting operations in Afghanistan.

killing Osama bin Laden, and then rooting out all terrorist networks across the world. It was time for the U.S. Army to go into action.

U.S. ARMY SPECIAL OPERATIONS FORCES

On October 21, 2001, the U.S. Joint Chiefs of Staff confirmed that U.S. Army special forces and elite Rangers were engaged in pitched battles with the Taliban inside Afghanistan. The first battles took

U.S. Army involvement in Afghanistan includes humanitarian as well as combat operations. Here, Lieutenant Laurie Green, a platoon leader with the U.S. Army's 92nd Engineer Battalion, helps an Afghan child try on a new coat donated by schoolchildren from the U.S.

place at Al Qaeda's spiritual stronghold of Kandahar, in the southeast of the country, and at an airfield 60 miles (96 km) away. U.S. Rangers took the airfield in a ferocious, 30-minute gun battle, while special forces soldiers assisted friendly Afghan units, known as the Northern Alliance, in taking Kandahar. On December 7, Kandahar fell to the Allies.

U.S. Special Forces have been in action in Afghanistan continuously since late October 2001, alongside other elite forces, including the British Special Air Service (SAS). Much about their operations is not known, because these elite troops value their anonymity and operational privacy. So what do we know of the U.S. Special Forces soldiers, and how will they fight terrorism?

U.S. Army Special Operations Forces (SOF) soldiers come under the jurisdiction of the U.S. Army Special Operations Command. The soldiers under its command fall into the categories of:

- Special Forces Groups (SFG)
- Rangers
- Special Operations Aviation
- Psychological Operations

A U.S. Army special forces soldier hands out new uniforms and equipment to recruits from the Afghan National Army at their training site in Kabul. In 2002, approximately 200 special forces soldiers were deployed in Afghanistan to equip and train members of the local army.

- Civil Affairs
- Signal and Combat Service Support

They also include the counterterrorism unit, Delta Force, more accurately known as Special Forces Operational Detachment Delta. Delta Force is a distinct part of the special forces. Usually, Special Forces units are organized according to Operational Detachments A and B. Often, five "A teams" will be commanded by one "B team." The main combat groups are as follows.

Operations in Afghanistan were often conducted at an altitude of over 10,000 feet (3,280 m), where even walking is exhausting. Here, two soldiers of the 101st Airborne Division take a break during Operation Anaconda, although they keep their weapons at the ready in case of an enemy ambush.

OPERATION ANACONDA

At the time of this writing, U.S. SOF are engaged in Operation Anaconda, named after the snake that slowly constricts its prey to death. It has involved heavy fighting with Al Qaeda and Taliban terrorists around Gardez in the mountainous eastern region of Afghanistan. The operation began on March 2, 2002, when U.S. aircraft dropped more than 450 bombs on suspected enemy positions. SOF troops and soldiers from the 101st Airborne and 10th Mountain divisions were then helicoptered into the region and immediately faced heavy resistance. One unit of the 10th Mountain Division fought a 20-hour gun battle with the enemy. An MH-47 Chinook helicopter was hit by a rocket-propelled grenade (RPG), and another MH-47 was also shot down. These incidents resulted in the deaths of seven U.S. soldiers, and another soldier was killed in a firefight with Al Qaeda rebels.

However, the losses to the Afghan opponents numbered in the hundreds. U.S. SOF troops blasted out Al Qaeda fighters from their mountainous positions using antitank rockets, and also captured **mortars**, RPGs, rifles, and ammunition. The Taliban and Al Qaeda fighters were forced to withdraw.

Commenting on the action, President Bush remarked: "I'm obviously saddened by the loss of life. On the other hand, I think most Americans...understand the cause is important and the cause is just. Our country is still under threat and so long as our country is under threat, this great nation will hunt down those who want to harm innocent Americans."

SPECIAL FORCES GROUPS

There are currently eight known SFGs, with approximately 1,400 men in each group—women are currently not allowed to join the special forces. According to official SOF publicity, "The mission of the Special Forces Groups is to plan, prepare for, and when directed, deploy to conduct unconventional warfare, foreign internal defense, special reconnaissance, and direct actions in support of U.S. national policy objectives within designated areas of responsibility."

Rangers

The U.S. Army Rangers are a large formation of elite infantry. Their main role is to capture key terrain or destroy enemy positions in hostile environments, often in places well beyond large-scale Army support. The Rangers are specialists in airborne and mountain warfare, making them ideal for missions in places like Afghanistan.

160th Special Operations Aviation Regiment

A unique unit of pilots trained to deploy or extract SOF soldiers during missions behind enemy lines. They also conduct reconnaissance missions and, in certain circumstances, combat air strikes.

Delta Force differs slightly from the others. It was created in the late 1970s under the authorization of ex-President Jimmy Carter.

Right: U.S. reserve troops conduct a training exercise in Dublin, California. Here, they are rappelling down a 40-foot (13-m) tower. Since September 11, 2001, Army reserve forces have put themselves in constant readiness to respond to any further terrorist attacks.

The war against terrorism is as much fought from surveillance consoles as it is on the battlefield. Modern satellite and airborne surveillance systems give U.S. Army troops "real time" information— they see events unfolding on their computers as they happen.

While the countries of Europe had already established their own counterterrorist organizations, the United States lagged behind, mainly because the U.S. mainland did not suffer from terrorist attacks. Delta Force was created in 1977 to plug this gap by the former SOF commander Colonel Charles Beckwith. Since its foundation, Delta Force has fought in many wars and actions, including deployments in the Gulf War, Somalia, and the former Yugoslavia.

U.S. Special Forces are among the most highly trained soldiers in the world. All SOF recruits must already be serving as soldiers with exemplary records of service. The SOF training program lasts up to a year, and during that time, about 80 percent of the recruits will fail the course. Would-be Rangers attend the demanding Ranger school, while SOF recruits go to John F. Kennedy Special Warfare Center in Fort Bragg, California. (Because he was fascinated by unconventional warfare, President Kennedy was the force behind the creation of the original 5th Special Forces Group in Vietnam in the 1960s.)

During SOF training, recruits will be put through physical tests that push their endurance to the limit, but they will also learn skills not taught to the regular soldier. These skills include engineering, foreign languages, medicine, intelligence gathering, sabotage, demolitions, advanced communications, survival, and escape and evasion.

Those soldiers that do pass recruitment are ideally suited to counterterrorist warfare. They can act alone in isolated places, regardless of the terrain or weather. When a terrorist base is identified, they can hit it hard with maximum firepower. SOF snipers can take out terrorist leaders from distances of more than 3,048 ft (1,000 m). They can also track down terrorists using expert tracking and surveillance skills.

Such are the qualities currently being used in Afghanistan, and which will be used throughout the world in the battle against terrorism. At home, 7,685 reservist soldiers were brought into active service to protect the U.S. homeland as part of Operation Noble Eagle. These soldiers are currently guarding important places.

The U.S. Army soldier is part of an elite group that will be relentless in its war against terrorism. The road ahead will undoubtedly be hard, but the determination to succeed will not falter.

GLOSSARY

Anthrax: a bacterial disease of sheep and cattle, which can infect, and kill, human beings

Ballistic: of or relating to firearms

Barracks: a building or set of buildings used especially for lodging soldiers

Bayonet: a steel blade attached at the muzzle end of a rifle or similar weapon and used in hand-to-hand combat

Cold War: a state of hostilities short of outright war that existed from 1945 to the late 1980s between the communist Soviet Union and the United States and its allies

Communism: a system in which goods are owned in common and are available to all as needed

Conscription: compulsory enrollment of persons especially for military service

CS gas: a caustic gas that makes the eyes sting and water and makes breathing painful

Democracy: government by the people; especially, rule of the majority

Insurgent: a person who revolts against civil authority or an established government

Kit: the equipment that a soldier has to carry into combat, including a backpack, ammunition, and weapon

Logistics: the aspect of military science dealing with the procurement, maintenance, and transportation of military materiel, facilities, and personnel

Materiel: equipment, apparatus, and supplies used by an organization or institution

Militia: a military force raised from civilians, which supports a regular army in times of war

Monocle: an eyeglass for one eye

Mortar: a muzzle-loading cannon used to throw projectiles at high angles

NATO: North Atlantic Treaty Organization; an organization of North American and European countries formed in 1949 to protect one another against possible Soviet aggression

Ordnance: military supplies, including weapons, ammunition, combat vehicles, and maintenance tools and equipment

Pyrotechnic: relating to various combustible or explosive devices

Scud: a Russian-made ballistic missile used heavily by Iraq during the Gulf War

Truce: a suspension of fighting by agreement of opposing forces

UN: United Nations; an international organization, of which the United States is a member, that was established in 1945 to promote international peace and security

CHRONOLOGY

1775: June 14, the Continental Army is formed, the first army of the United States.

1775–1783: The Continental Army fights in the Revolutionary War, helping to free the United States from British rule; it is officially disbanded on November 2, 1783, and thereafter becomes the U.S. Army.

1787: The U.S. Constitution is written; President George Washington becomes the Army's commander-in-chief.

1812–1815: The U.S. Army fights against the British in the War of 1812.

1812: West Point Military academy is established.

1846–1848: The U.S. Army fights and wins the Mexican-American War.

1861–1865: The U.S. Civil War; the Union Army eventually defeats the Confederate Army.

1916: The National Defense Act authorizes the Army to expand to 175,000 men in 111 regiments.

1917–1918: The U.S. Army enters World War I as part of the American Expeditionary Force led by General John J. Pershing; soldier numbers reach nearly four million men.

1940: Conscription is introduced, bringing the U.S. Army to a strength of 1.6 million men.

1941: December 7, the Japanese attack Pearl Harbor, and the United States enters World War II.

1945: September, World War II officially ends; over 11 million U.S. Army soldiers have served during the war.

1947: The U.S. Army Air Force splits away from the Army to become the U.S. Air Force.

1950–1953: The U.S. Army goes to war again, this time in Korea as part of an international UN army against the Communists.

1961–1973: The U.S. Army becomes steadily involved in the Vietnam War.

1973–1990: The U.S. Army conducts combat missions and peacekeeping operations in areas around the world, including Grenada, the Middle East, and Panama.

1990–1991: In the biggest mission since Vietnam, the U.S. Army forms a massive part of an Allied force that liberates Kuwait during the Gulf War.

1995–: U.S. troops conduct peacekeeping and humanitarian operations in the territories of the former Yugoslavia, Europe.

2001–: U.S. special forces fight the Al Qaeda terrorist network in Afghanistan and prepare for more international operations in the war against terrorism.

FURTHER INFORMATION

USEFUL WEB SITES

U.S. Department of Defense: www.defenselink.mil

U.S. Army main Web site: www.army.mil

U.S. Army recruitment site: www.goarmy.com

National Guard: www.arng.army.mil

Reserve Officer Training Corps: www.armyrotc.com

U.S. Army weapons: usmilitary.about.com/cs/armyweapons/

FURTHER READING

Beckwith, Charlie A. and Donald Knox. *Delta Force: The Army's Elite Counter-Terrorist Unit.* London and New York: Avon, 2000.

Bowden, Mark. *Blackhawk Down: A Story of Modern War.* New York: Signet, 2000.

Harclerode, Peter and Mike Dewar. *Secret Soldiers: Special Forces in the War Against Terrorism.* New York: Cassell Academic, 2001.

Kurtz, Henry. *U.S. Army.* Brookfield, Connecticut: Econo-Clad Books, 1999.

Nelson, Harold (editor). *The Army.* Southport, Connecticut: Hugh Lauter Levin Associates, 2001.

Netanyahu, Benjamin. *Fighting Terrorism: How Democracies Can Defeat Domestic and International Terrorists.* New York: Noonday Press, 1997.

U.S. Department of the Army Handbook. New York: International Business Publications, 2001.

RECRUITMENT INFORMATION

To become a full-time regular soldier in the U.S. Army, you need to be between the ages of 17 and 35, a U.S. citizen or registered alien, and in good physical shape. For the Army Reserve, the criteria are the same, except that the upper age limit is reduced to 34. Army officers are recruited through a university or college participating in the Reserve Officer Training Corps, the Officer Candidate School, or the United States Military Academy at West Point. To enquire about any of these opportunities, go to a local army recruiting office or visit the Web site www.goarmy.com.

ABOUT THE AUTHOR

Dr. Chris McNab has written and edited numerous books on military history and the world's elite military forces. His list of publications to date includes *The Illustrated History of the Vietnam War, German Paratroopers of World War II, The World's Best Soldiers, The Elite Forces Manual of Endurance Techniques,* and *How to Pass the SAS Selection Course.* Chris' research into these titles has brought him into contact with many of the world's elite units, including the U.S. Marines and British Special Forces. Chris has also contributed to the field of military technology with publications such as *Weapons of War: AK47, Twentieth Century Small Arms,* and *Modern Military Uniforms.* His editorial projects include *The Battle of Britain* and *Fighting Techniques of the U.S. Marines 1941–45.* Chris lives in South Wales, U.K.

INDEX